EARTH WATCH

Written by

Penny Horton, Tony Potter and Dee Turner

Illustrated by

Jackie Harland, Robin Lawrie, Shelagh McNicholas and Guy Smith

Designed by

Teresa Foster

Edited by

Tony Potter

Environmental consultants

Peter Berry, Director, The Conservation Trust

Steve Pollock, BBC Education Officer

CONTENTS

About this book

Earth Watch looks at major problems facing the planet: rising population, pollution, dwindling resources, poverty and the destruction of wildlife. Each problem is introduced by pages of background information. These are followed by a detailed case history to give you a closer look at the subject.

These are the topics and their case histories:

Planet Earth

How the Earth works: the delicate balance of air, land and sea that enables life to survive on the planet. Why are these conditions now threatened?

1 Population

How fast is the world population rising? What can be done about it?

Case study: China

How has China dealt with its population problems?

2 The Third World

What is the Third World, and what are the problems faced by people who live there?

Case study: Bangladesh

What is it like to be poor in one of the most overcrowded and disaster-prone areas of the world?

3 Resources

Many of the Earth's natural resources are being used up and cannot be replaced. What can be done about this?

Case study: Oil

Where does oil come from? How is it used? What are the problems involved in using it as a fuel?

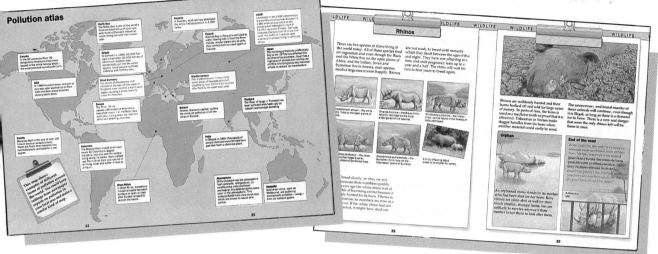

4 Pollution

How are people polluting the air, water and land on the planet? What is the greenhouse effect? What can individuals do to help?

Case study: **Pollution atlas**

Where are the pollution trouble spots of the world?

5 Wildlife

How are humans threatening the survival of plants and animals? What can be done to protect wildlife?

Case study: **The black rhino**

Why do people hunt the rhino? How can it be protected?

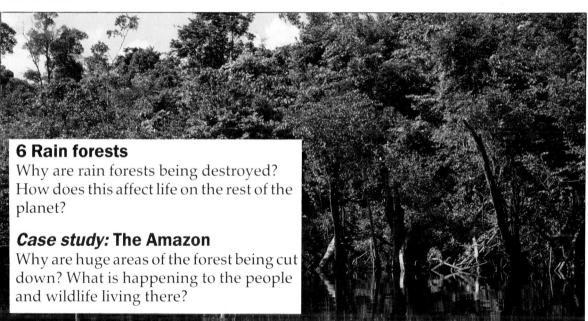

6 Rain forests

Why are rain forests being destroyed? How does this affect life on the rest of the planet?

Case study: **The Amazon**

Why are huge areas of the forest being cut down? What is happening to the people and wildlife living there?

What can you do to help?

There *are* things you can do to help protect life on Earth. Ideas for them are given throughout this book. On page 47 there is a list of organizations that can give you further information and advice.

ENVIRONMENT FRIENDLY

Planet Earth

Earth is the only known planet in the Universe with human and animal life. It is one of nine planets orbiting the Sun, itself a minor star near the edge of our galaxy. The galaxy is only one of millions so far detected in the universe.

To get an idea of how tiny Earth is in the vastness of space, imagine that the planet were the size of the picture on this page. On this scale, the Sun would be 57km away and Alpha Centuri, the nearest star, would be over 10,000km away.

Earth is home to countless millions of different kinds of plants and animals, each of which has evolved over thousands of years to survive in different habitats. The planet and its inhabitants are threatened by the activities of just one species – man. Some examples of the destruction are shown on these two pages.

Agricultural chemicals may damage the soil and end up in our water and food supply.

Earth time clock

Planet Earth is 4,600 million years old. Imagine this time condensed into twelve hours – Earth began at 8 o'clock this morning and it is now 8 o'clock at night. The pictures below show what has happened during the course of the day.

8.00am — **9.50am**	Nothing much is known about the Earth during the first hour and fifty minutes.
9.50am — **7.00pm**	Scientists have pieced together evidence to find information about the development of the Earth's atmosphere, continents and rocks during the first eleven hours.
6.57pm	The first flowering plants appeared.
7.44pm	Dinosaurs and reptiles evolved just 16 minutes ago.
7.50pm	The first mammals arrived ten minutes ago.
7.59pm	The first man-like creatures appeared 20 seconds ago.
7.59pm	Modern man, homo sapiens, developed just five seconds ago.
7.59pm	Agriculture was discovered just over a second ago.
7.59pm	The industrial revolution began about one five-hundredths of a second ago – the time it takes a camera to take a photograph.
8.00pm	Today.

The seas are being polluted by industrial chemicals and untreated sewage.

Habitats are being destroyed to make way for roads, housing and farmland for the world's ever-increasing population.

The world today

During the last second of the imaginary Earth time clock, Earth and its inhabitants are gradually being damaged and destroyed by its most successful mammal – man.

Most of the damage to the environment has occured during the "camera flash" since the industrial revolution began in the 18th century. Before this time, man-made destruction usually affected only a limited local area, such as the clearing of forests to make ships, for example. Since the industrial revolution the effects of activities such as fuel burning and manufacturing processes have become more and more global.

About 500 species of animals have been made extinct through hunting and destruction of their habitats.

The atmosphere has been polluted by car exhausts, factory and power station emissions.

The soil is being polluted by household and industrial waste, in dumps called landfill sites.

The planet has been pillaged for raw materials — coal, oil bauxite (to make aluminium), iron ore and so on.

The biosphere

The biosphere is the name given to the layer of soil, water and air upon the surface of the Earth. All living things are also part of the biosphere. These four parts each have special names, and you can find out about them over the next six pages:

- air is called the atmosphere.
- water is called the hydrosphere.
- the soil and rocks are called the lithosphere.
- living things are called the ecosphere.

What happens in one part of the biosphere affects what happens in another part.

This picture shows the layers of the Earth's interior.

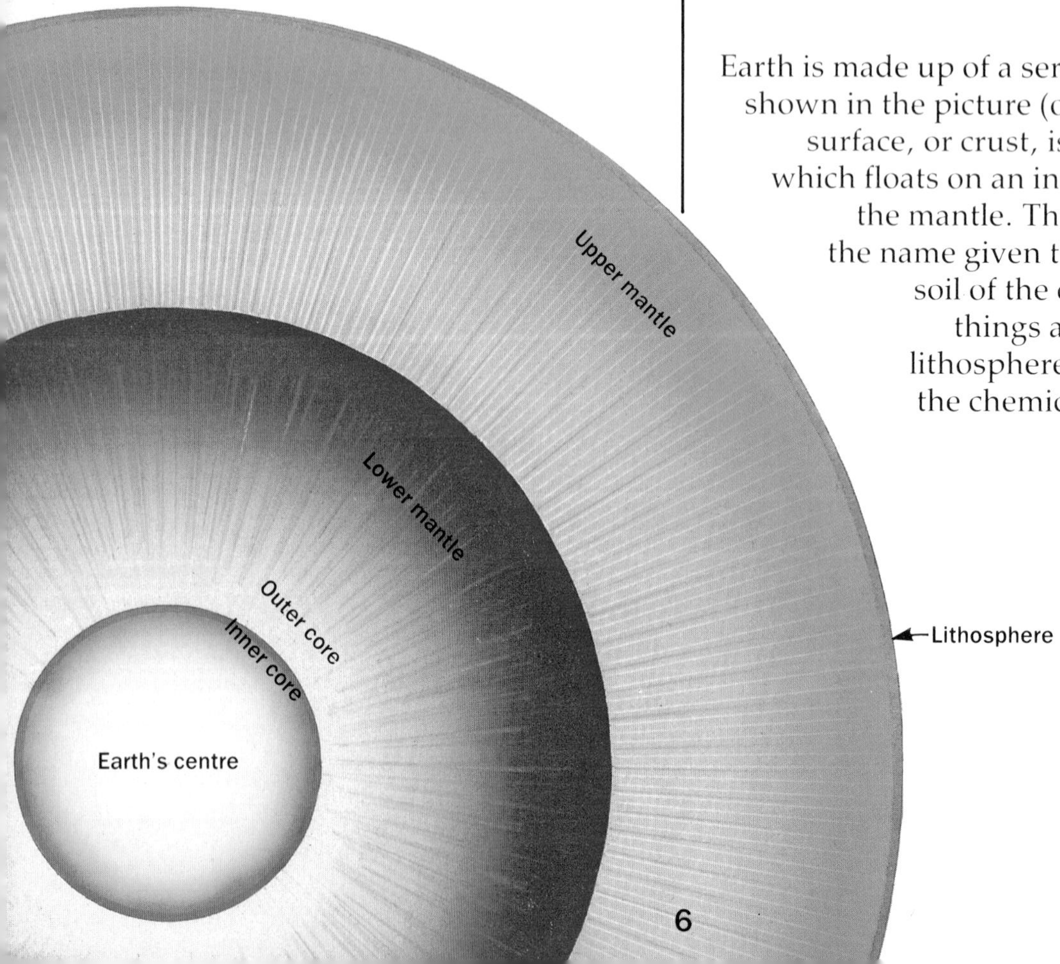

The lithosphere

The biosphere is a very thin skin around the Earth. Imagine Earth the size of a football. The biosphere would only be the thickness of a coat of paint on the surface of the ball.

Earth is made up of a series of layers, as shown in the picture (on the left). The surface, or crust, is a layer of rock which floats on an inner layer called the mantle. The lithosphere is the name given to the rocks and soil of the crust. All living things are found in the lithosphere. It contains all the chemical components of life.

Upper mantle

Lower mantle

Outer core

Inner core

Earth's centre

←Lithosphere

How rocks were formed

Rocks have been formed over millions of years in three basic ways.

Igneous rocks

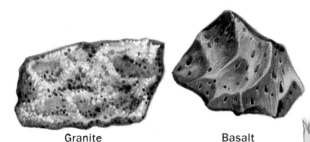

Granite   Basalt

Granite and basalt are examples of igneous rocks – a type of rock which cooled from molten lava, usually from a volcano. They contain important minerals and metals.

Sedimentary rocks

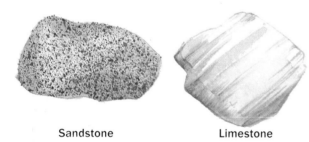

Sandstone   Limestone

This kind of rock was formed by different materials, such as sand, clay and plant remains, gradually settling on top of one another, usually under water. All fossil fuels (oil, coal and gas) and many building materials come from sedimentary rocks.

Metamorphic rocks

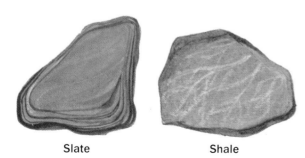

Slate   Shale

Metamorphic (Greek for "change") rocks have been changed by heat or intense pressure. Slate, for example, is clay compressed to make shale, which in turn is compressed to make slate.

How soil is made

The upper layer of the lithosphere is soil. Soil is made from tiny particles of rock which have been broken down over thousands of years by rainwater, gases in the atmosphere, ice, tree roots and by decaying plants and animals.

It would take about 23,000 years to produce soil the depth of this page. →

Plant life

Plants cannot grow without soil, and without plants there would be no animals. Soil provides the moisture and nutrients, or food, for plants to grow.

Fertile soil

The most fertile soils in the world are where there are no extremes of climate and where there is plenty of decomposing vegetable matter, called humus. The climate of a region affects the kind of soil there. In very wet areas, for example, the moisture may wash important minerals from the soil.

Only about ⅕ of the world's land surface has fertile soil.

Soil erosion

Soil erosion is when the top layer of soil is washed or blown away, leaving only infertile ground below. Soil is usually protected by the trees and plants which grow in it, but if they are removed then the soil is exposed to the weather. Soil erosion happens all round the world, and for different reasons.

- **Britain**   Digging up hedgerows
- **Amazon**   Destruction of trees
- **Sahara**   Overgrazing by cattle
- **Australia**   Ploughing of unsuitable areas

BIOSPHERE 2

The atmosphere

The atmosphere is a layer of gases that surrounds the Earth. The gases are held in place by gravity. Without the atmosphere there would be no air for plants, humans and other animals to breathe, so there would be no life on the planet.

The atmosphere protects the planet. It shields Earth from the Sun's dangerous rays. It also burns up space debris such as meteors so that, usually, they do not crash into Earth and damage it. The moon and other planets in the solar system are not protected by an atmosphere like this.

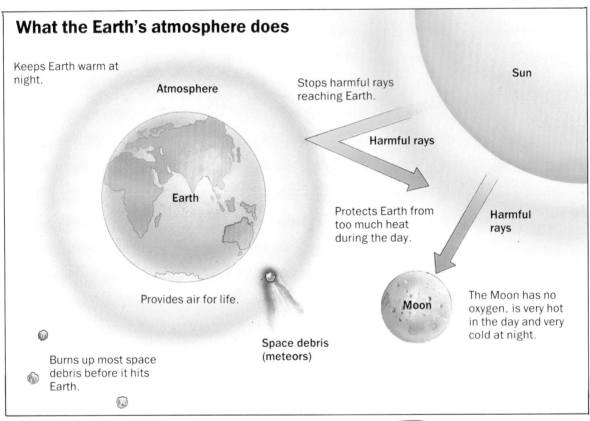

What the Earth's atmosphere does

Keeps Earth warm at night.

Atmosphere

Stops harmful rays reaching Earth.

Sun

Harmful rays

Earth

Harmful rays

Protects Earth from too much heat during the day.

Provides air for life.

The Moon has no oxygen, is very hot in the day and very cold at night.

Moon

Space debris (meteors)

Burns up most space debris before it hits Earth.

What air is made of

Air is a mixture of gases that cannot be seen or smelled. Most of the gas in the air is nitrogen. About one-fifth is oxygen. There are also small amounts of carbon dioxide and argon, and tiny amounts of other gases. Animals breathe oxygen. Plants breathe in carbon dioxide.

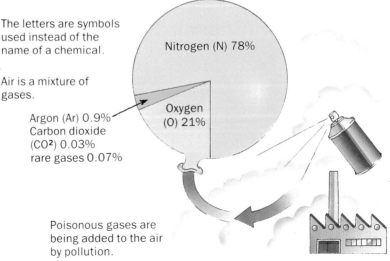

The letters are symbols used instead of the name of a chemical.

Air is a mixture of gases.

Argon (Ar) 0.9%
Carbon dioxide
(CO_2) 0.03%
rare gases 0.07%

Nitrogen (N) 78%

Oxygen (O) 21%

Poisonous gases are being added to the air by pollution.

Changes in the atmosphere

Billions of years ago, the atmosphere was quite different from today's. There was little oxygen. There was much more carbon dioxide than there is today.

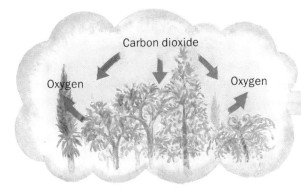

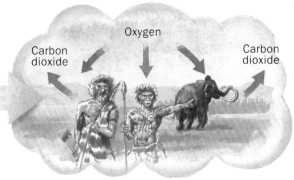

When trees and plants began to grow on Earth, they changed the atmosphere by taking in carbon dioxide and giving out oxygen into the air.

As oxygen levels rose, tiny oxygen-breathing animals developed. All fish, insects, birds and other animals developed from them.

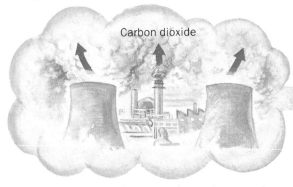

Now the atmosphere is changing again. So much coal and oil have been burned in the last 150 years that levels of carbon dioxide in the air are rising.

Destroying forests means there are fewer trees to use up the carbon dioxide. All life could be damaged by these changes in the atmosphere.

The hydrosphere

The hydrosphere is all the water on Earth. It is needed by all living things. Water is constantly being recycled, going from ocean to air to land and back to the ocean. This is called the water cycle and is shown in the picture on the right. About 97% of the Earth's water is in the ocean.

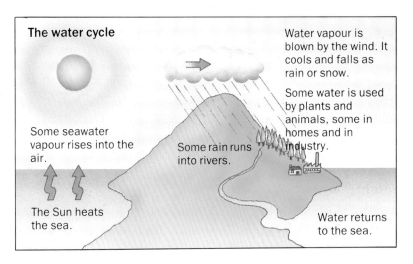

The water cycle

Water vapour is blown by the wind. It cools and falls as rain or snow.

Some water is used by plants and animals, some in homes and in industry.

Some seawater vapour rises into the air.

Some rain runs into rivers.

The Sun heats the sea.

Water returns to the sea.

BIOSPHERE 3

The ecosphere

Living things did not appear on Earth until about 3,000 million years ago – 1,600 million years after the planet was formed. The ecosphere is the name given to all these living things – all plants and animals. Now there are millions of different kinds of living things. Each plant or animal has its own special place in the ecosphere. Each has adapted to suit a particular habitat – the part of the world where it lives.

Flamingoes have adapted to life in the water. Their long legs enable them to wade in the shallows.

Plant life

Plants appeared on Earth first. They make their own food, using soil, water, energy from the Sun, and carbon dioxide from the air. This process is called photosynthesis. When the food is made, the plant gives off oxygen into the air. Plants recycle the gases in air. They also provide food for animals.

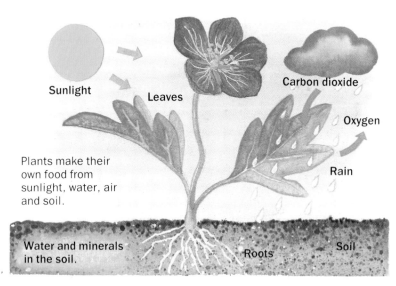
Sunlight

Leaves

Carbon dioxide

Oxygen

Rain

Plants make their own food from sunlight, water, air and soil.

Water and minerals in the soil.

Roots

Soil

Plants make their own food from sunlight, water, air and soil.

Animal life

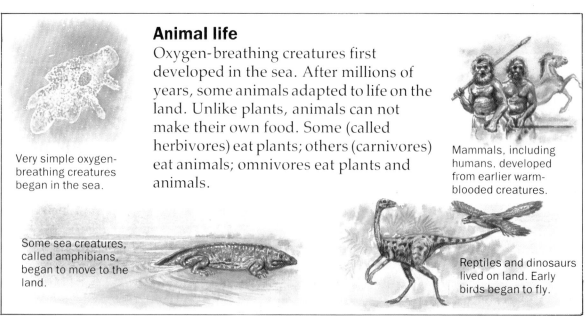

Oxygen-breathing creatures first developed in the sea. After millions of years, some animals adapted to life on the land. Unlike plants, animals can not make their own food. Some (called herbivores) eat plants; others (carnivores) eat animals; omnivores eat plants and animals.

Very simple oxygen-breathing creatures began in the sea.

Mammals, including humans, developed from earlier warm-blooded creatures.

Some sea creatures, called amphibians, began to move to the land.

Reptiles and dinosaurs lived on land. Early birds began to fly.

Ecology

This is the study of the way living things exist together and depend on each other. If one part of the biosphere is damaged or changed, this affects other parts. Because plants and animals need food to give them energy, all the living things in an area are linked together in a food chain. A food chain begins with plants and ends with meat-eaters.

Food chain

In this woodland the living things provide food for each other. Some animals feed on plants. Some animals eat other animals. Other living things break down dead animals and plants. The remains rot into the soil, and help the plants to grow.

Owls eat voles and (occasionally) birds.

Foxes eat rabbits and voles.

Robins eat caterpillars.

Rabbits eat green plants.

Voles eat grass, worms and (occasionally) caterpillars.

Caterpillars eat dead leaves.

Green plants make their own food.

Insects, funghi and worms eat dead plants and animals and help them rot into the ground.

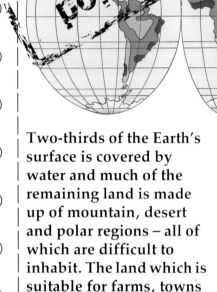

Human Population

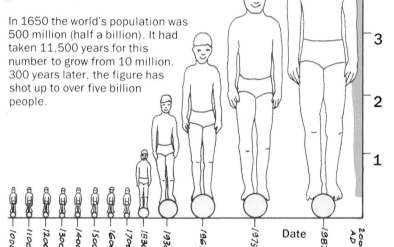

In 1650 the world's population was 500 million (half a billion). It had taken 11,500 years for this number to grow from 10 million. 300 years later, the figure has shot up to over five billion people.

Two-thirds of the Earth's surface is covered by water and much of the remaining land is made up of mountain, desert and polar regions – all of which are difficult to inhabit. The land which is suitable for farms, towns and cities is under pressure from an ever-increasing population.

Births and deaths

The rapid increase in population is due to a drop in the death rate. The balance between births and deaths has been disturbed mainly because of improved health care during the last 100 years, especially in wealthy countries. Far fewer babies die of diseases and people live for much longer.

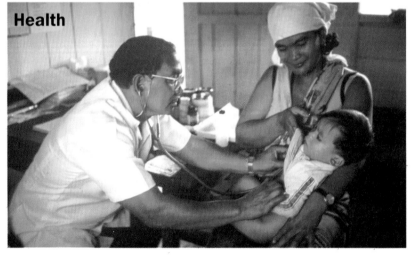

Health

Health care has improved in the Third World, but many babies still die of starvation or disease. Many poverty stricken families have a lot of children in the hope that some will grow up and be able to help support the family Western families tend to have fewer children because they know that their children are likely to survive.

Population problems

World over-population has created many problems including housing shortages, a rise in unemployment, the loss of raw materials and fuels which can never be replaced, and the pollution and destruction of wildlife.

Many areas of poorer countries are on the verge of starvation, while other developed countries have food surpluses. Food production will have to double by the year 2020 to keep the world's rising population from hunger.

Cities

Since the industrial revolution in the 18th century, fewer people have been needed to farm the land. People gradually moved from the countryside into the cities to the new factories. This trend has continued, so that today one quarter of the population lives in the world's 25,000 cities.

Unemployment is often high in cities, so many people end up jobless and homeless.

Land

As land is cleared for people, wildlife and their habitats are often destroyed – usually forever.

In Dorset 80% of the heathland has been used up in the last 200 years.

Solving the population problems

The rate at which the world's population is increasing has to be controlled. Many experts believe that the best way of doing this is by making sure that the world's poor are able to feed and care for themselves. Better family planning and health care in poor countries will help couples to have fewer children. To increase food production, cash crops need to be replaced by food crops. Cash crops, such as tobacco, tea and coffee, do not feed the local people but are grown to sell to developed countries.

China

The Chinese population is about one fifth of the world total, at just over one billion people. This is expected to rise to one and half billion by 2020. The Chinese government faces the problem of feeding, housing, clothing, teaching and employing all these people. One of the ways it has tackled the problem is by trying to control the population increase.

China covers 9,957,000 square kilometres – enough space to fit Spain into 18 times! Much of the country, the Gobi desert, for example, is uninhabitable. The more fertile areas and cities are very crowded.

The one-child policy

In 1980, in an attempt to reduce the population, the Chinese government introduced a policy to persuade parents to have only one child. These parents receive a higher salary, better housing and better education for their only child, compared to parents with more children.

Families who have more than one child get less pay, worse housing and poorer educational opportunities.

In cities the government seems to have succeeded in its aim – in 1987 96% of couples in Shanghai having their first baby agreed to make it their last. But the government seems to have had little success in the countryside.

A good idea?

Can you imagine what it would be like if the government tried a one-child policy here? Would you agree? See if you can think of reasons for and against the Chinese idea.

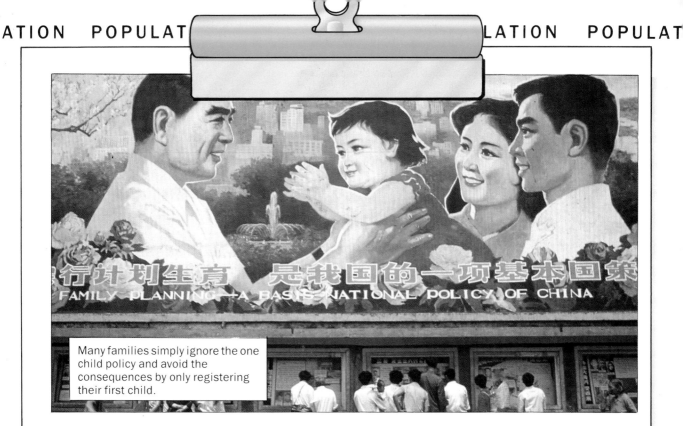

FAMILY PLANNING—A BASIS NATIONAL POLICY OF CHINA

Many families simply ignore the one child policy and avoid the consequences by only registering their first child.

Boys and girls

Rural families need several children, to help on the land and to ensure a good chance of survival. It is important to Chinese families that a son is born so that he can take on family responsibilities when the parents die.

The one-child policy offers no chance to "try again" if a girl is born, so it is generally accepted that rural families will "keep trying" until a son is born.

Planning a family

All over the world, Family Planning Associations help couples choose the number of babies they have. They teach people about sex education and help them to look after their young children.

In May 1980 the China Family Planning Association (FPA) was set up as a voluntary organization to teach families about contraception and birth control to achieve fewer, but healthier, babies.

By law, all unmarried couples in China must be advised by the FPA. This has helped to reduce the amount of unwanted pregnancies in this group.

The China FPA was awarded a gold medal in November 1988 by the Better World Society, based in Washington, USA, for its outstanding family planning work.

The Third World

The Third World is the name given to the poorest countries. Three quarters of the people on Earth live in the Third World. Because they are so poor, these people have to face many problems. Another name for the Third World is the underdeveloped, or developing countries.

The Third World countries are coloured red on this world map. They include Mexico, Central America and most of South America, all of Africa except the south, and most of the Middle East and Asia.

Problems of the Third World

The biggest problem of the Third World is lack of money. Because these countries are so poor, many people are hungry, unhealthy and live in bad housing conditions.

Agriculture

Most people are farmers but poor soil and out-of-date techniques mean they cannot grow enough to feed everyone.

Education

Only about half the children get any education, and most of them leave before secondary school. Fewer than 20 people in 100 can read.

Resources

There is very little coal, oil or gas so the main source of fuel is wood. But supplies of wood are dwindling as the forests are cut down.

Population

The number of people in the Third World is rising very fast. So more people are competing for the small amount of food, land and resources.

Health

Poor diet, unclean water and bad housing cause disease and illness and there are very few doctors. In Britain there are about 860 people to one doctor. In India there are 5,000 people and in Indonesia 27,000 people to each doctor.

Life expectancy

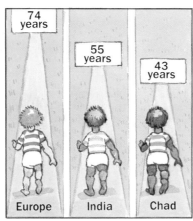

74 years

55 years

43 years

Europe India Chad

These are the average number of years that people can expect to live in Europe, India and Chad (in Africa).

Trade and industry

Most Third World countries were once colonies belonging to the rich countries. Now their trade is still controlled by the developed world. Their factories often belong to big multi-national companies based in the rich countries.

Floods

Disasters

As if the poorest countries did not have enough problems, many of them are in parts of the world where disasters often occur.

Drought

Cyclones

Earthquakes

Pests

Wars

What is being done to help?

The governments of the rich countries give some money to the Third World, but it is not nearly enough to solve its problems. International organisations such as the United Nations work to help the poorer nations.

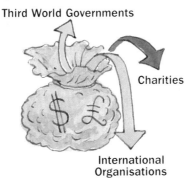

Third World Governments

Charities

International Organisations

Charities collect money from people who want to help. Bandaid concerts collected millions. Oxfam and Save the Children Fund help improve farming and health. They also set up small factories where people can make goods and earn money.

Bangladesh

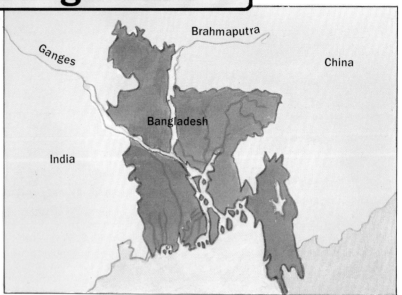

Bangladesh is a very poor country, with too many people, not enough food, great poverty and frequent natural disasters.

Flooding

Bangladesh has suffered terribly from floods that wash away people, homes, animals and crops. This is partly because it is a low lying country full of huge rivers that drain into the sea. In this part of the world, cyclones happen, with heavy rain and high winds whipping up the sea and sending tidal waves over the land.

And the flooding is getting worse. This is because so much of the forest in the Himalayas, in India and Nepal, is being cut down. Soil washes down from the deforested area, blocking up rivers and sending even bigger floods down into Bangladesh. In 1987, one million houses were washed away in floods after heavy rain. Many people died and crops were lost.

Population

Bangladesh is one of the poorest and most over-crowded countries in the world. The population rises by 2 million every year. Its biggest problem is to slow down this population growth.
If growth isn't stopped, there will be 206 million people in Bangladesh by the year 2020. This is as crowded as having most of the population of the USA living in England.

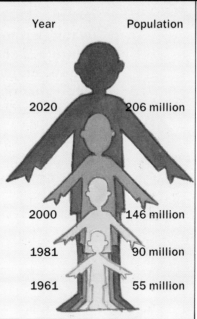

Year	Population
2020	206 million
2000	146 million
1981	90 million
1961	55 million

Health

Health is poor and many suffer from malnutrition. There is one doctor for every 9,700 people.

Water

There is plenty of water in Bangladesh but only 40 people in 100 have clean water to drink.

Education

For every 20 children, only 12 go to school. Of those, only two boys and one girl will go on to secondary school. And only one of them will go on to further education. Girls receive less education than boys because of the religious beliefs of the country. 43% of men can read, but only 22% of women. Girls usually marry at about 12 or 13.

Farming

The soil is good for rice growing, but crops often fail and farming methods are out of date. Most people work in farming, but own no land of their own.

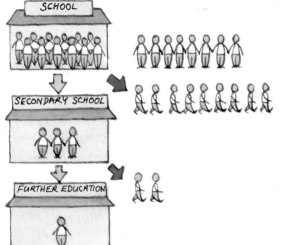

What is being done?

Almost 100 relief agencies work with the poor in city slums and rural areas.

Resources

Natural resources are all the things that the Earth provides and which are used by people. They include heat, light, air and water, without which life could not continue. They also include soil and plants, animals on land and in the seas, and valuable minerals and fossil fuels buried under the ground.

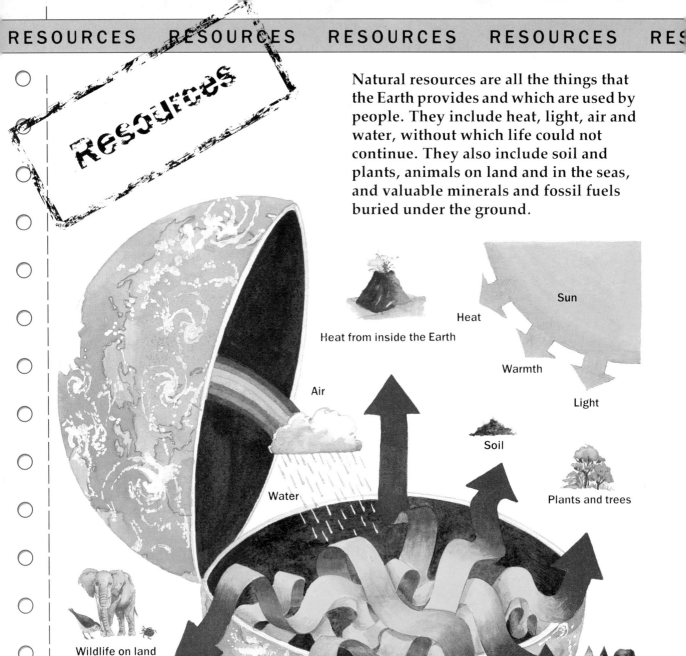

Heat from inside the Earth

Heat

Sun

Warmth

Light

Air

Water

Soil

Plants and trees

Wildlife on land

Wildlife in the sea

Fossil fuels

Minerals and metals

The world's resources

The Earth has a population of over 5 billion, and each day that number rises by almost 250,000. This means that natural resources are in great demand to feed, clothe, house and transport people.

Some resources, such as fossil fuels, are being used up quickly and cannot be replaced. Others, such as plants and animals, can renew themselves, but need to be protected if they are to thrive.

Renewable resources

Renewable resources are those which should never run out. For example, plants and animals reproduce themselves, while soil, water and air are naturally recycled. But the pressure of human use is now threatening these precious resources. Pollution is a major enemy. So, too, is the destruction of natural habitats such as forests.

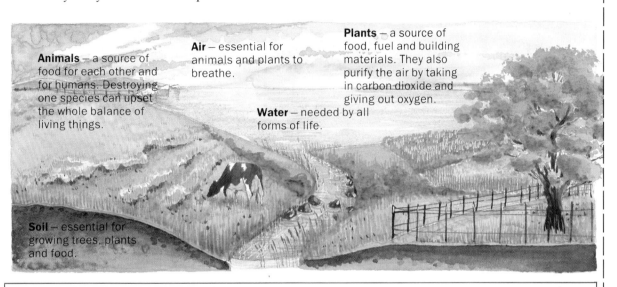

Animals – a source of food for each other and for humans. Destroying one species can upset the whole balance of living things.

Air – essential for animals and plants to breathe.

Plants – a source of food, fuel and building materials. They also purify the air by taking in carbon dioxide and giving out oxygen.

Water – needed by all forms of life.

Soil – essential for growing trees, plants and food.

Recycling and reusing

Some resources can be used again and again. Metal, glass and paper can be broken up and made into new items. This saves using new raw materials and the energy which would otherwise be used to process them. Here are some things you can do to save resources.

Don't throw cans away. Collect aluminium drinks cans and sell them to scrap merchants.

Magnets will not stick to aluminium.

950 million tin cans a year are recycled in the UK. Most are picked up by huge magnets that sort through rubbish. Some are collected in skips.

Put glass bottles into bottle banks. They can be melted down and made into new bottles.

Reuse bags, boxes and envelopes.

The average UK home contains 17 plastic carrier bags. Reuse them – don't get new ones each time you shop.

Take bags and cartons back to shops for reuse.

Put labels on used envelopes.

Non-renewable resources

Some of the Earth's resources cannot be replaced. These include the minerals, coal, oil and gases found in the Earth's crust. The rich countries of the world are using these resources up so fast that before long there will be none left. Many of these resources are used to produce energy, such as electricity.

Energy

The rich countries use huge amounts of fossil fuels – gas, oil and coal – to make electricity, heat homes, light streets and buildings, work electric gadgets, fuel cars and power machines in factories.

Energy resources are unequally shared. The USA has only 6% of the world's population, but uses 30% of its energy. India has 20% of the world's population, but uses only 2% of the world's energy.

As much coal has been used in the last 40 years as was used in the whole of history before then.

Oil and gas supplies may run out in about 40 years time, and coal in 100 years.

China, the USA and the USSR together contain more than half the world's supply of coal.

Fossil fuel energy is a major source of pollution. Gases given off by cars, power stations and factories, poison the air and produce damaging acid rain (see page 30).

Coal began to be used about 300 years ago. Oil and gas were not used until about 100 years ago.

Oil is the world's largest source of energy.

Fossil fuels were formed millions of years ago when tiny plants and animals in the sea died. Their bodies were trapped under mud and rocks and pressed down until they turned into coal, gas and oil. They took millions of years to form and cannot be replaced.

Running out of energy

Fossil fuel resources are running out, so it is important to discover how to use less energy. It is also essential to find alternative ways of making energy, using non-polluting sources such as Sun, wind and water power.

Conserving energy

A great deal of energy is wasted. In an energy-efficient future, new techniques and attitudes will be needed to cut out waste and conserve (save) power. Energy-saving houses will be needed, with good insulation and microchip-controlled heating and lighting. Petrol guzzling cars are being replaced by cars with more efficient engines. Better public transport would cut down car use, unblock roads and make air cleaner. Factories could re-use waste heat and produce goods that are energy-efficient.

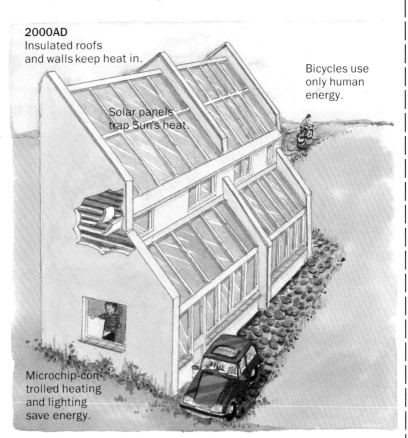

2000AD
Insulated roofs and walls keep heat in.

Bicycles use only human energy.

Solar panels trap Sun's heat.

Microchip-controlled heating and lighting save energy.

Renewable energy

Energy can be made from sunlight, wind and water. There is an endless supply of these resources and they do not pollute the planet.

The Sun's energy can be used directly to heat houses and water, and to make electricity.

Windmills can harness the wind's power to drive machines, or produce electricity.

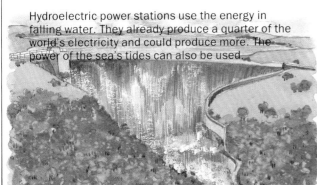

Hydroelectric power stations use the energy in falling water. They already produce a quarter of the world's electricity and could produce more. The power of the sea's tides can also be used.

Geothermal energy (heat from the Earth's core) can be harnessed to produce energy and electric power.

Oil

Oil is energy from the Sun, trapped inside tiny creatures that lived under the sea millions of years ago. When they died they became covered in sedimentary rock. Eventually, the hydrogen and carbon atoms that made up their bodies turned into hydrocarbons forming oil and gas. Different kinds of animals and plants produced different kinds of oils.

People often imagine crude oil is found in a huge, thick, black lake under the ground. In fact it is held in tiny droplets in the rock like drops of water in a sponge. It smells sweet and looks rather like cough medicine.

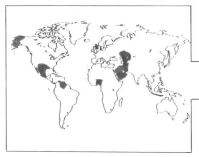

Oil is found mostly in North America, the USSR and the Middle East, which has over half the world's known oil supply.

Geologists look for oil in areas where the right kinds of rock are found. They drill holes deep into the rock.

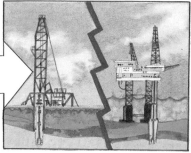

If enough oil is found there, an oil company will build a well to bring it to the surface. Oil rigs bring oil up from under the sea.

Oil is then taken by pipeline or tanker to a refinery. There it is heated to 300°C and broken down into many separate ingredients.

Propane and butane gases, petrol, naphtha, aircraft fuel, paraffin, diesel, gas oils and lubricating oil are all made from crude oil.

Oil by-products include plastics. animal feeds, artificial fibres, paint, fertilizers, cosmetics, preservatives and drugs.

How much oil is used?

About 2.8 billion tonnes of oil are used each year throughout the world. As much as one half is used in transport. About one-third is used in cars and lorries.

How long will oil last?

The oil already discovered will last for about another 30-40 years. Even with new reserves being discovered, it will probably run out in 60 years.

Alternatives to oil

Scientists are experimenting with new ways of powering cars. They are looking for energy that uses renewable resources and does not pollute the air. They have tried using electricity, gases and alcohol as fuels.

Some experimental cars run on energy from the Sun. This electric car is solar powered.

Car fuel

In Brazil, half a million cars run on alcohol made from plants. Swedish scientists have tried to make alcohol fuel from willow trees. In the USA fuel has been made from corn. Hydrogen may be an alternative fuel for cars in the future.

Pollution

Oil pollution is damaging the oceans. Each year about 200,000 tonnes of oil leak into the sea from terminals where ships collect or deliver their oil cargoes. Huge amounts of oil waste are deliberately dumped at sea. There are also accidents, when oil leaks from a tanker or pipeline as it is being transported. The oil does not dissolve in the water but forms a layer on top that blocks out light and air. Wildlife in the sea suffers, and oil-covered birds and animals die. When the *Exxon Valdez* tanker spilled 35,000 tonnes of oil into the sea off Alaska in March 1989, more than 34,000 birds and 10,000 sea otters were among the wildlife victims. 4,800 sq km of ocean were polluted.

Recent spillages in Britain

January 1988 9,000 gallons of oil spilled into the sea in Belfast.

April 1988 The Thames was polluted for 8km when a lorry crashed.

August 1989 8km stretch of the River Tamar polluted by fuel oil.

August 1989 150 tons of crude oil leaked from a pipeline into the River Mersey polluting 30km of coastline.

September 1989 Two tankers collided near the River Humber, sending out a large oil slick.

Seabirds, like this one, die if they get oil on their feathers unless treated quickly.

Pollution means making the Earth's air, land and water dirty with substances which would not naturally be in the environment. All the things people use, from cars to washing-up liquid, are likely to cause pollution at some point in their manufacture or use. Some of the substances used in making things eventually break down into harmless chemicals when thrown away. These are called biodegradable substances, and include things such as paper and fabrics. Other things, such as plastics, are usually not biodegradable.

Natural waste, such as sewage, will usually be treated with bacteria which makes it harmless. If too much untreated sewage is dumped into rivers or seas, it will poison animals and many forms of marine plants, even killing them.

The air you breathe, the water you drink and the land where your food is grown may be polluted by various substances, such as artificial fertilizers, toxic fumes and waste.

Acid rain, which is caused by sulphur dioxide and nitrogen oxides from factories and vehicle exhausts, damages trees, buildings and wildlife.

Oil slicks and chemicals from factories are killing fish and animals living in or near seas, rivers and lakes.

Chemicals from crop spraying stay in the soil and are washed into water supplies making water in some areas unfit to drink.

Chemical and nuclear dumps store dangerous waste which eventually pollute the surrounding area.

People are poisoned by chemicals in food.

Trees die from the acid in acid rain and chemicals in the soil.

Litter pollution

Litter is any rubbish that does not find its way to a wastepaper bin, dustbin or rubbish dump.

Litter pollution creates many dangers to the environment and is usually caused by people wanting to dispose of their rubbish as easily as possible with little or no thought for the ugliness or dangers they are creating.

Over half the world's litter pollution is created by rubbish that escapes from homes, shops, offices and industry, as well as building sites. Some litter is also blown by the wind from dumps.

The rest is created by pedestrians and motorists dropping rubbish in the streets and throwing it out of car windows.

Litter dangers

Listed below are some of the hazards caused by litter.

- Abandoned cars create dangers for children playing nearby.
- Cigarette ends and matches cause fires.
- Bottles trap and kill small animals.
- Broken glass, ring pulls and food cans cut both people and animals.
- Plastic bags and cups can suffocate or choke grazing cattle.
- Dog and cat mess, if touched by young children, can cause blindness.

What you can do

Make sure that your rubbish is safely disposed of. This may take a bit more time and effort, but it is your own surroundings, where you live, work and play that you will be protecting.

Find out if there are any facilities for recycling in your area. Paper, glass and some fizzy drink cans can all be used again, so find out from your local council how you can help.

Make your own recycled paper

You will need:

Old newspaper

A bucket

A washing-up bowl

Powder paint

A wooden spoon

A piece of wire mesh

Dishcloths

A plastic bag

Plenty of heavy books

1 Old newspaper — Soak overnight in water.

2 Drain off water.

3 Powder paint — Put into a bowl. Mash into a pulp and add colour.

4 Mix in the same volume of water.

5 Slide the wire mesh into the pulp.

6 Lift out the mesh covered with pulp.

7 Clean surface — Dishcloth — Press down hard, then remove the mesh.

8 Heavy books — Dishcloth — Plastic bag — Pulp under cloth

9 Leave for several hours until the pulp dries and becomes paper. Remove the books, plastic bags and cloth, and peel up gently.

10 Newspaper — Paper — Leave the paper until it is completely dry and ready for use.

The greenhouse effect

When coal and other natural fuels are burned and when plants, trees and other living things die and rot away, a gas called carbon dioxide is released into the atmosphere.

As the Sun's heat reaches Earth some is absorbed by plants, trees and the oceans, while a great deal bounces back into the atmosphere. As it does so, the carbon dioxide in the air traps some of this heat.

Water vapour evaporating from seas, rivers and lakes also absorbs the Sun's heat.

Since the Industrial Revolution, the levels of carbon dioxide have increased rapidly. Even so, carbon dioxide today only accounts for a small percentage of the Earth's atmosphere. But it is enough to begin a warming of the Earth which could result in some drastic changes.

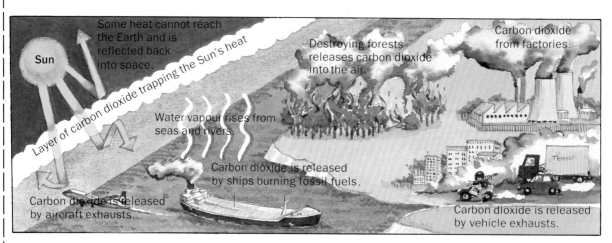

Sun — Some heat cannot reach the Earth and is reflected back into space. Layer of carbon dioxide trapping the Sun's heat. Water vapour rises from seas and rivers. Carbon dioxide is released by aircraft exhausts. Carbon dioxide is released by ships burning fossil fuels. Destroying forests releases carbon dioxide into the air. Carbon dioxide from factories. Carbon dioxide is released by vehicle exhausts.

Melt down

A 4°C increase in the climate, which has been predicted to take about 150 years, could melt the ice at the North and South Poles. The map below gives an idea of how little land the world would be left with if this were to happen.

The planet Venus is about the same size as the Earth but is closer to the Sun. A greenhouse effect has resulted in a ground temperature of 477°C. An increase in carbon dioxide, which now accounts for 95% of the planet's atmosphere, traps most of the Sun's heat.

Reducing carbon dioxide

By burning less wood, oil and coal the levels of carbon dioxide reaching the atmosphere would reduce. This would mean relying on other sources of power such as wind, water or the Sun.

The burning and cutting down of rain forests accounts for a great deal of the carbon dioxide released into the atmosphere, making it a major contributor to the greenhouse effect. If this destruction stopped, carbon dioxide levels would be nearly halved.

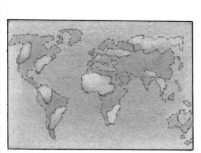

The ozone layer

Between 10 and 15 kilometres above the Earth's surface lies a thin band of gas called ozone.

This protects the Earth from the Sun's harmful, ultra-violet rays, which are known to cause skin cancer. But the ozone can only be made with the help of ultra-violet rays. So in parts of the world where there is a lot of sunlight, there is more ozone in the atmosphere.

This was a very efficient natural cycle, until man-made chemicals and gases began to destroy the ozone.

Ozone destroyers

The main destroyer of ozone is a gas called chlorine. This is combined with other chemicals to make chlorofluorocarbons (CFCs) in industry, and chloromethane in nature. When these two chemicals are released into the atmosphere and reach the ozone layer, ultra-violet rays break them down, releasing the chlorine which destroys the ozone.

The dangers

If the ozone layer con-tinues to be destroyed more and more people will become victims of skin cancer through exposure to ultra-violet rays.

If ozone is not there to trap ultra-violet rays, they will add to the global warming already being caused by the greenhouse effect.

In 1985, scientists noticed a 'hole' in the ozone layer above Antarctica. Since then, international efforts have been made to control damage to the ozone layer by reducing the use of these chemicals and gases.

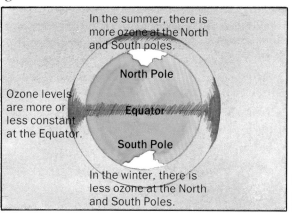

In the summer, there is more ozone at the North and South poles.

North Pole

Ozone levels are more or less constant at the Equator.

Equator

South Pole

In the winter, there is less ozone at the North and South Poles.

CFCs are used in aerosol cans, refrigeration, air-conditioning units and plastic foam packaging. CFCs account for less than half of the chlorine that is destroying the ozone layer.

Chloromethane is released from rotting vegetation, manure and indigestible gases. As the population increases, these natural processes accelerate giving off dangerous amounts of gas.

What can you do?

Look for "ozone friendly" labels on many products which used to contain CFS.

Many companies now label their products so that they you know they are "environment friendly".

29

Water pollution

The world's water is being poisoned by sewage and chemicals from industry and farming. Accidents, such as oil spillages at sea, also add to the problems.

Rain, too, is becoming more and more polluted. Acid rain kills water creatures, damages buildings and destroys trees.

Water pollution is a threat to all life on Earth, especially in the rivers, lakes and seas of heavily populated areas such as Japan and Europe.

Acid rain

Gases, such as sulphur dioxide and nitrogen oxides, and small particles from power stations and car exhausts, are dissolved in rainwater. This turns rain, hail or snow into a dilute acid – often as strong as lemon juice.

Acid rain eats into the stonework of buildings. This medieval gargoyle has been badly damaged.

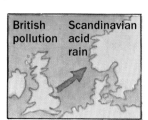

British pollution   Scandinavian acid rain

Pollution from one country is often blown by the wind to make acid rain in a neighbouring country.

Oil spillages

Damaged oil tankers leak oil into the sea, poisoning ocean life. Sea birds are killed or injured by the oil clogging their feathers. They can no longer keep warm, fly or feed themselves and eventually die.

Oil from the *Exxon Valdez* caused catastrophic damage to the coastline of Alaska in 1989.

Some sea birds are rescued and cleaned with detergents, but have to be looked after until the natural oils in their feathers are restored.

Farming

Rain washes pesticides and artificial fertilizers used in farming from the land into rivers and seas. These chemicals are eaten by animals and fish. People can be affected by eating contaminated food, or by drinking polluted water that has accidentally entered the water supply.

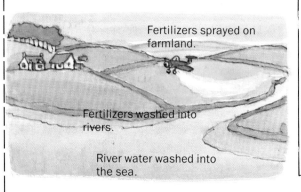

Fertilizers sprayed on farmland.

Fertilizers washed into rivers.

River water washed into the sea.

What you can do

Here are a few practical things to do to help reduce the amount of acid rain-producing chemicals in the atmosphere.

Coal-burning power stations are a major source of electricity and acid rain. Try to make an effort to switch off unwanted lights.

Even if your family car runs on unleaded petrol, its exhaust still produces damaging chemicals. Try walking or cycling instead of going by car.

Some cars are beginning to be fitted with catalytic converters — "cats" for short — which cut out dangerous exhaust gases. You could write to one of the big car manufacturers to see if their new models will be fitted with "cats".

Nuclear power

Nuclear power is an alternative energy source to oil, coal and gas – the fossil fuels. It uses uranium, found in some kinds of rock, as a fuel. This is radioactive, which means that its atoms constantly break down, giving off harmful rays of energy. Some kinds of uranium produce three million times as much energy as the same amount of coal.

Nuclear power stations use radioactive fuel to heat water. This makes steam, which in turn is used to drive giant electricity-generating turbines.

Radioactivity

Fuel such as uranium produces extremely dangerous radioactive rays during the process of making nuclear power. The fuel is shielded by lead and concrete to prevent the rays from escaping and harming anyone. Radioactivity damages living cells and can cause cancer.

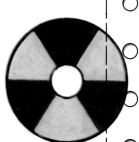

This symbol is used to show that something is radioactive.

Nuclear pollution

Nuclear power stations cause pollution in several ways, shown in the pictures below.

Nuclear waste

Some nuclear power stations are cooled by water, which can become radioactive. Waste water is sometimes pumped into the sea, which many experts believe is dangerous.

Waste

When nuclear fuel is used up, it is stored underground or at sea. The waste is still dangerous – some fuels remain radioactive for millions of years. Scientists disagree whether or not storage is safe over such long periods of time.

Safer power

Scientists are working on renewable energy sources – those that don't use up resources such as coal and which avoid damage to the environment. Ideas include wind and wave power.

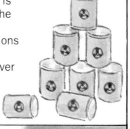

Wind power generator

Accidents

The world's worst nuclear accident was in 1986 when part of a nuclear plant exploded in Chernobyl, USSR. A radioactive cloud spread over Europe, but no one yet knows how much damage has been caused.

The inside of the Chernobyl nuclear power station before the explosion.

Pollution atlas

North Sea
The North Sea is one of the world's most polluted areas of open sea, with much of Europe's industrial waste being dumped into it each year.

Canada
In the St Lawrence River 30 dangerous chemicals have been traced in the white beluga whale — the most polluted mammal on Earth.

Britain
In Cornwall in 1988, 60,000 fish were killed when 20,000 tonnes of aluminium sulphate was accidentally put into the water system. Local people suffered sickness and memory loss.

USA
In 1988 hospital waste dumped at sea was later washed up on New York and New Jersey beaches, closing them down.

West Germany
The levels of phosphates and nitrates in the sea off the coast of Friesland have created a build-up of algae, causing a sticky foam to cover the beaches.

Europe
The River Rhine carries 100 tonnes of poisonous industrial waste into the North Sea each year, killing sea birds, fish and other sea-dwelling creatures.

Pacific
Mururoa Atoll is the site of over 130 French nuclear weapons tests. There are fears that radiation has harmed people and wildlife in the region.

Colombia
The Bogota River is used as an open sewer by Colombia's largest industrial complex and the people living along its banks. Many people use the river as their sole source of drinking water and suffer illness as a result.

This map shows examples of different forms of pollution around the world. You could keep cuttings from newspaper reports on pollution in your local area and make a similar kind of map.

West Africa
In West Africa, poisonous industrial waste has been dumped at open air tips after Europe refused to accept the waste.

32

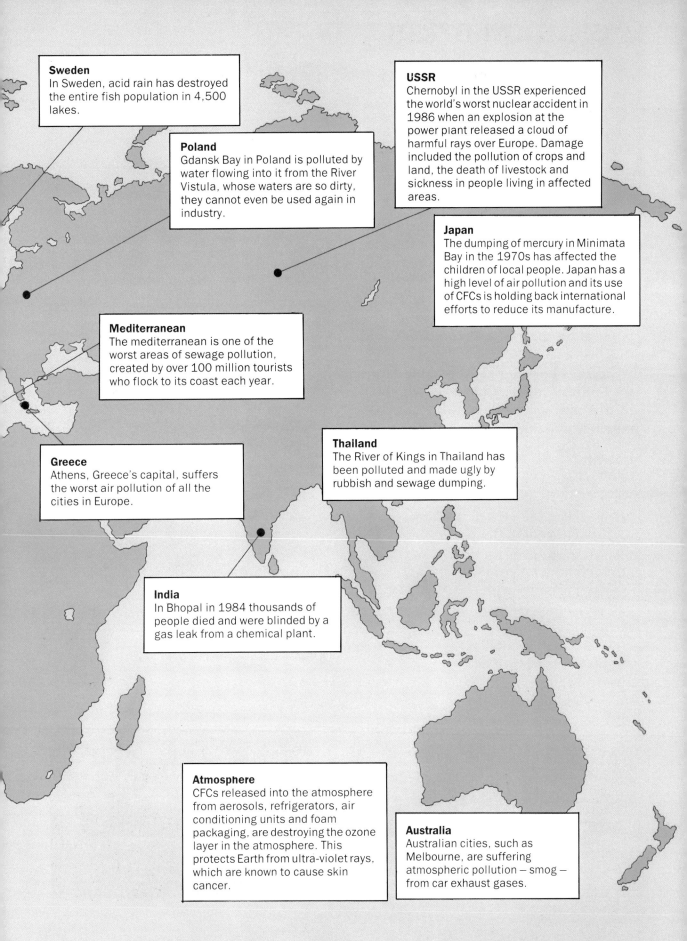

Sweden
In Sweden, acid rain has destroyed the entire fish population in 4,500 lakes.

Poland
Gdansk Bay in Poland is polluted by water flowing into it from the River Vistula, whose waters are so dirty, they cannot even be used again in industry.

USSR
Chernobyl in the USSR experienced the world's worst nuclear accident in 1986 when an explosion at the power plant released a cloud of harmful rays over Europe. Damage included the pollution of crops and land, the death of livestock and sickness in people living in affected areas.

Japan
The dumping of mercury in Minimata Bay in the 1970s has affected the children of local people. Japan has a high level of air pollution and its use of CFCs is holding back international efforts to reduce its manufacture.

Mediterranean
The mediterranean is one of the worst areas of sewage pollution, created by over 100 million tourists who flock to its coast each year.

Greece
Athens, Greece's capital, suffers the worst air pollution of all the cities in Europe.

Thailand
The River of Kings in Thailand has been polluted and made ugly by rubbish and sewage dumping.

India
In Bhopal in 1984 thousands of people died and were blinded by a gas leak from a chemical plant.

Atmosphere
CFCs released into the atmosphere from aerosols, refrigerators, air conditioning units and foam packaging, are destroying the ozone layer in the atmosphere. This protects Earth from ultra-violet rays, which are known to cause skin cancer.

Australia
Australian cities, such as Melbourne, are suffering atmospheric pollution – smog – from car exhaust gases.

Wildlife

As the world population increases the people of the world need more food to eat, more space to live and more fuel to burn for energy. The world's wildlife needs food and space too, but as the human population grows the wildlife population suffers loss of land, and with it, a loss of food sources. The world's wildlife is increasingly threatened by the homelessness and hunger which results, but sadly this is only one aspect which is endangering their future.

As more and more of the countryside is taken over to build new towns, the animals that lived naturally in the wild lose their homes and must struggle to find new ones, or to adapt to their new surroundings.

Hunting

Early people killed animals for food but because they only killed what they needed, the wildlife population was not threatened. People lived in harmony with nature. Then when people started hunting animals for pleasure and not just for food, the balance was upset and the struggle for survival began.

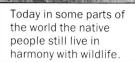

Today in some parts of the world the native people still live in harmony with wildlife.

In North America nearly all the North American bison were hunted and killed. If a reserve had not been set up to protect and breed the last few, these bison would no longer exist.

1989 International ban on trading of ivory

The world's elephants are under serious threat of extinction due to their brutal murder to obtain their ivory tusks, which are sold for large sums of money.

Passenger pigeons were killed by the million each year until there were none left and the bird became extinct.

The Blue Morpho butterfly of the tropical rain forests is hunted and killed to be sold for use in jewellery and other forms of decoration. There are also butterfly collectors all over the world who will pay high prices for the Blue Morpho because of its stunning beauty. Sadly, where there is a demand for something, money can be made and so capture, death and trade of these butterflies will continue until this demand stops.

Blue morpho

Homeless

If an area of woodland is cut down to make way for farm buildings and fields all these creatures, plants and trees lose their natural home.

As well as the dangers of hunting, wildlife is also a victim of homelessness. The home of each animal, its habitat, is destroyed by people changing the land to suit their own needs. As more factories, houses and roads are built, wildlife is forced to move away or is killed. Even turning wildlife habitats into farmland reduces the amount of wild animals that can live there.

Once an area has been taken over and used to build factories, there is little hope that wildlife will be able to survive there.

In Britain, over the last 45 years, the common frog's numbers have been reduced dramatically. This is because drainage ditches, dewponds and wetlands which are the natural home for the common frog have been filled in to make way for buildings and farmland. Without these areas frogs have nowhere to breed. Then a study found that frog communities were thriving in back garden ponds. You could build a pond at home or school and save homeless frogs.

How to build a pond

You will need:

A spade
Some large stones
Plastic sheeting
Old rags
Straw
Soil
Old pond water (tap water will do)
Pond weeds

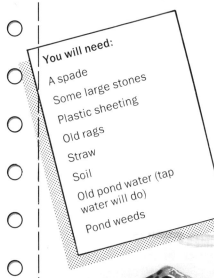

2m
1m
Ledges   Sloping sides

1. Dig a hole about 2 metres wide and 1 metre deep with sloping sides and ledges.

Large stones round the edges to hold the plastic in place.

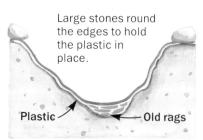

Plastic   Old rags

2. Put rags in the bottom to cover any sharp sticks and stones and line the hole with plastic.

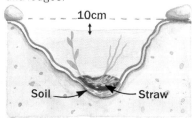

10cm
Soil   Straw

3. Fill with old pond water to about 10 centimetres from the top. Add some soil, straw and weeds.

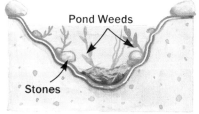

Pond Weeds
Stones

4. Put stones at the bottom and on the ledges for animals to shelter and to get in and out of the pond.

Pollution

Pollution from oil, chemicals and smoke, poisons habitats and kills wildlife. As long as people keep polluting the environment, wildlife is in danger. Some countries are now taking steps to reduce pollution, but without world co-operation pollution will continue to take lives.

Pollution not only affects individual animals but all related members of the food chain. If a small insect is poisoned, the bird that eats it will be poisoned too. This is very real problem the world over, for example, for birds of prey, from ospreys in North America to peregrine falcons in Britain.

Food chain.

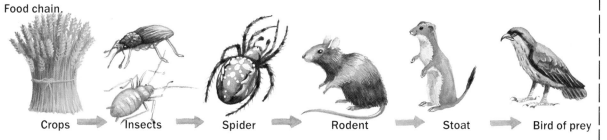

Crops ⟶ Insects ⟶ Spider ⟶ Rodent ⟶ Stoat ⟶ Bird of prey

Pesticides

In the 1950s and '60s, a pesticide called DDT was widely used on crops to kill off pests. The crops were eaten by rodents who took an amount of this long-lasting poison into their bodies. Birds ate insects living on the crops with the same result. When peregrine falcons in Britain caught and ate the birds and rodents, pesticide was passed on to them.

As a result of eating this poison, the female peregrines were not able to produce enough calcium to make their eggshells strong. The young peregrines growing inside the eggs could not survive. When this was realised DDT was banned. Today, by law, pesticides must only be active long enough to kill crop pests. This is intended to stop other creatures from being poisoned, but the danger is still there during these short periods.

Rhinos

There are five species of rhino living in the world today. All of these species feed on vegetation and even though the Black and the White live on the open plains of Africa, and the Indian, Javan and Sumatran live in forests, each species needs a large area to exist happily. Rhinos are not ready to breed until maturity which they reach between the ages of five and eight. They have one offspring at a time and each pregnancy lasts up to a year and a half. The rhino will wait for two to four years to breed again.

Ceratotherium simum — the white rhino, lives on the open plains of Africa.

Diceros bicornis — the Black rhino, recently recorded as the most endangered of the species.

Rhinoceros unicornis — the Indian rhino, can be found in the forests of India and Nepal.

Rhinoceros sondaicus — the Javan rhino, another forest dweller, inhabits areas of Southeast Asia.

Dicerorhinus sumatrensis — the Sumatran rhino lives on the Indonesian island of Sumatra.

A rhino offspring stays close to its mother for safety.

Rhinos breed slowly, so they are not able to increase their numbers quickly. Fifteen years ago the white rhino was at serious risk of becoming extinct because it was widely hunted for its horn. Thanks to conservationists its numbers are now at a healthy level. If the white rhino had not been protected, it might have died out.

Rhinos are ruthlessly hunted and their horns hacked off and sold for large sums of money. In parts of Asia, the horn is used as a medicine (with no proof that it is effective). Tribesmen in Yemen make dagger handles from the horn when another material could easily be used.

The unnecessary and brutal murder of these animals will continue, even though it is illegal, as long as there is a demand for its horn. There is a very real danger that soon the only rhinos left will be those in zoos.

Orphan

An orphaned rhino stands by its mother who has been shot for her horn. Baby rhinos are often shot as well for their much smaller, stumpy horns, but are unlikely to survive anyway if their mother is not there to look after them.

End of the road

Zoos could be the only way to save animals such as rhinos from extinction. Nature reserves with armed guards to protect the animals from poachers are another solution. What do you think should be done?

A rhino in a zoo.

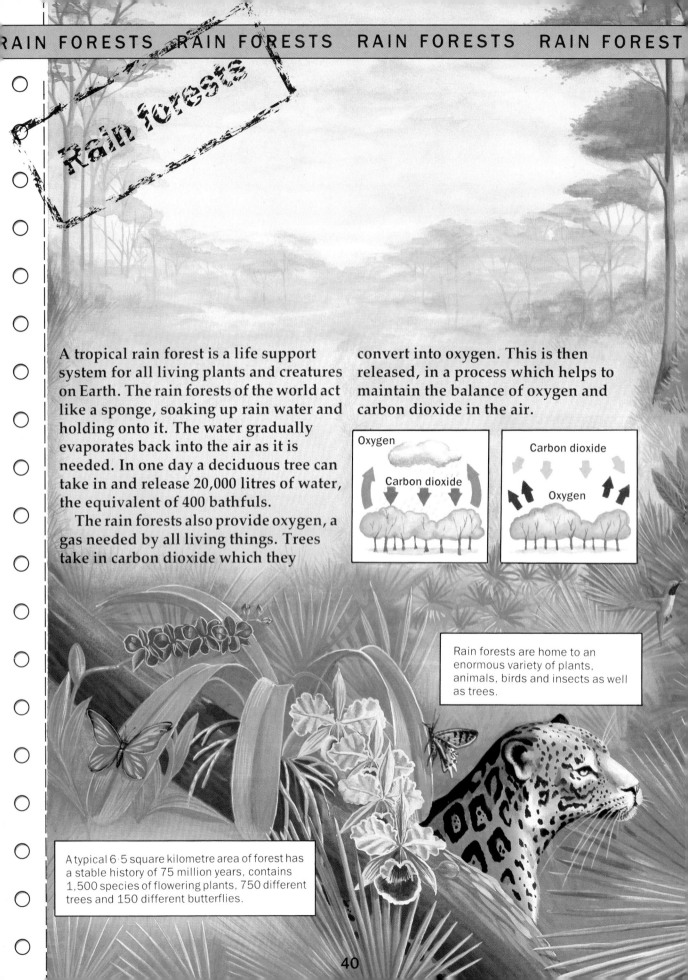

Rain forests

A tropical rain forest is a life support system for all living plants and creatures on Earth. The rain forests of the world act like a sponge, soaking up rain water and holding onto it. The water gradually evaporates back into the air as it is needed. In one day a deciduous tree can take in and release 20,000 litres of water, the equivalent of 400 bathfuls.

The rain forests also provide oxygen, a gas needed by all living things. Trees take in carbon dioxide which they convert into oxygen. This is then released, in a process which helps to maintain the balance of oxygen and carbon dioxide in the air.

Rain forests are home to an enormous variety of plants, animals, birds and insects as well as trees.

A typical 6·5 square kilometre area of forest has a stable history of 75 million years, contains 1,500 species of flowering plants, 750 different trees and 150 different butterflies.

Some trees, such as mahogany, grow only in the rain forests. These provide hardwood timber to make furniture and other products.

Forest cures

The Madagascar periwinkle

Rain forests are home to about 155,000 of the 250,000 plant species known to the world. Many contain chemicals which can help cure diseases. The US National Cancer Institute has identified 3,000 plants which may help to produce a cure for cancer. The Madagascar periwinkle is already used in a treatment for leukaemia in children.

As many as eight out of ten of all known insects live in the rain forest. 41,000 kinds of insect were found in a study of the Peruvian rain forest, including 12,000 different kinds of beetles, for example.

Forest damage

No matter where you are in the world, the rain forests play a vital role in your life. Yet in the time it has taken you to read this page close to 100 acres of rain forest has been destroyed.

Problems

It is estimated that one square kilometre of forest is destroyed every 2.5 minutes, usually by deliberate burning – over one million acres a week. If destruction continues at the present rate, the rain forests of the world could disappear forever by 2050.

The forests are being destroyed at such a frightening rate to make way for farmland, fast-growing trees to be used in the paper, building and furniture industries and urban development. Timber production alone destroys 12.5 million acres a year.

The destruction not only means that we are in danger of losing these beautiful tropical forests, but also the peoples, animals and plants that make them their home.

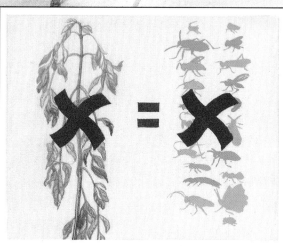

For every plant that becomes extinct through destruction there are an estimated 20 insects that will almost certainly not be able to survive without that plant.

Farming on land cleared in the rain forest is short-lived, but causes long-term damage. After only ten years, without the tree roots to hold the soil together, and plants and animals to keep it fertile, the soil will begin to break up and blow away as dust.

Atmospheric changes

Perhaps the most serious dangers created by forest destruction, which affect us all, are the changes made to the atmosphere and climate.

The burning and cutting down of the rain forests disturbs the Earth's water, carbon and oxygen cycles. Areas where rain forest no longer exists cannot take in water as before. As almost half the world's rain forest has been destroyed already, this has caused flooding, drought and changes in rainfall patterns. This change in the natural balance results in regional, even global, changes in the weather.

The more trees that are destroyed the less carbon dioxide they can convert into oxygen.

The mass burning of forest gives off vast amounts of carbon dioxide

Both these factors add to the already high levels of carbon dioxide caused by industry and vehicle exhausts in the developing world.

Solutions

Governments are now working to save what remains of the rain forests. These solutions are on a large scale and involve the co-operation of governments from many countries. But there are ways in which you can effect the future of the rain forests too. You could choose softwood products rather than tropical hardwoods – pine can be just as useful as mahogany, for example, and comes from forests which are renewed. But if you stopped buying rain forest products, what would happen to the poor peasants trying to make a living by selling them? Should you stop buying rain forest products, or support campaigns to have trees replaced?

● About four per cent of rain forest is under official protection in 560; preserved areas. This covers 780,000 square kilometres – an area the size of Turkey.

● Another two per cent (mostly in India) used for timber production is now managed to allow natural regrowth of the trees.

● Conservation deals have been set up. For example, Conservation International cancelled $650,000 of debt owed by Bolivia in return for government protection of 3.7 million acres of rain forest.

The Amazon

The rain forests of the Amazon region in South America are a staggering 75 million years old. In that time many different kinds of plants and animals have appeared and disappeared from the Earth. But many stayed and now there are more different kinds of plants and animals living in the rain forests of the Amazon than in any other part of the world. The Amazon River runs through this area of South America, taking with it millions of tonnes of water collected by the surrounding rain-soaked forest.

Forest tribes

The forest has also become home to tribes of South American Indians who only a few thousand years ago began to share the dense, moist forest with the plants and animals. They cleared small patches of land to grow their few crops and used the trees to build shelters. Using plants they made weapons and hunted animals such as monkeys for meat. They tipped their blow darts with poison from plants and colourful frogs.

Then when the land they had cleared was no longer fertile they would move on to another part of the jungle. Eventually, the area left behind would grow back.

About half a million of these native people still live in the forest, compared to four million in 1900. They continue to live in harmony with the forest, taking only what they need.

Money to burn

In Brazil, the country which the Amazon mostly occupies, there is pressure to make money to repay massive foreign debts – owed to western countries. Clearing the forest for timber and ranches is one way the Brazilians can earn money. In effect, the forest is converted into beef by clearing land to grow grass for cattle to graze. But once replaced by grass, the forest will never regrow and its animals and people will be lost. The scale of this destruction is staggering – on any given day in September 1988, for example, 8,000 fires were burning in the Amazon.

There is also pressure to exploit the minerals under the ground in the Amazon and to harness the power of the Amazon River for vast hydroelectric schemes. Many of these projects are funded by the World Bank and western companies.

What's to be done?

Countries such as Brazil are trying to change what is being done to the Amazon. One useful idea is a scheme to swap debts for guarantees to protect the forest. What do you think of this idea? You could try writing a letter to the Prime Minister to see what steps Britain is taking to help protect the Amazon.

* None of the burger chainstores in this country uses any rain forest beef.

18 square metres of rain forest is needed to raise enough beef for one hamburger*.

Rain forest products

This supermarket shelf shows things which are grown in rain forests. Should you buy them or not? What do you think?

Some people only buy hardwood furniture when they know it comes from an area where another hardwood tree has been planted in its place. You can find out which companies use this method from *The Good Wood Guide*, published by Friends of the Earth (address on page 47).

The future

The world contains enough food, fuel, and living space for everyone, provided the population can be kept at a reasonable level. But resources are unevenly spread. The rich countries are polluting the Earth. The poor countries suffer hunger and disease. At one time, aggression and selfishness helped humans defend themselves and survive. Now these instincts threaten the survival of the Earth. If there is to be a future for the planet, people will have to learn to work together, not fight.

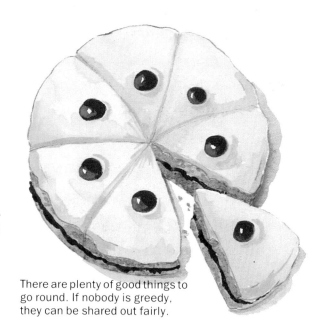

There are plenty of good things to go round. If nobody is greedy, they can be shared out fairly.

Funds for change

It will cost money to eradicate pollution, protect the environment, feed the hungry, improve health conditions and rehouse the homeless. Where will this money come from?

Individual contributions to charity.

Government money raised in taxes.

International funds from the World Bank and other development agencies.

Money saved by cutting back defence budgets.

During 1984, world military spending amounted to $1.4 million *per minute*!

Just 7 months' worth of defence spending could bring a clean water supply and sanitation to the 2 billion people on Earth who do not yet have these basic amenities.

What can you do?

The problems the Earth faces can only be solved if governments use their power and wealth to work together. But official attitudes will change only when there is a change in the attitudes of individuals. Everyone can make changes in their own life to help. Some ideas are shown below.

Campaign about local environmental issues.

Join a local conservation group, or set up your own.

Organize local recycling projects.

Avoid buying goods that harm the environment.

Make sure you know what is in the food you eat!

Encourage your family to save energy.
See how many more ideas you can think of.

These organizations can give you information and advice about what you can do to help planet Earth.

British Trust for
  Conservation Volunteers
36 St Mary's Street,
Wallingford,
Oxford OX10 0EU

World Wildlife Fund
Panda House
11-13 Ockford Road
Godalming
Surrey

Friends of the Earth
377 City Road
London EC1V 1NA

Oxfam
274 Banbury Road
Oxford OX2 7DZ

Save the Children Fund
Mary Dachelor House
17 Grove Lane
London SE5

National Centre for
  Alternative Technology
Llwyngwern Quarry
Machynlleth
Powys SY20 9AZ

The Conservation Trust
George Palmer Site
Northumberland Avenue
Reading
RG2 7PW

Royal Society for Nature
  Conservation
The Green
Nettleham
Lincoln LN2 2NR

Greenpeace
36 Graham Street
London N1 8LL

Intermediate Technology
103-105 Southampton Row
London WC1B 4HH

Earthlife
10 Belgrave Square
London SW1X 8PH

Index

Published by BBC Books, a division of BBC Enterprises Limited, Woodlands, 80 Wood Lane, London W12 OTT

First published 1990

© 1990 Times Four Publishing Limited/BBC Enterprises Limited

Devised and produced by Tony Potter for BBC Enterprises Limited

Paperback ISBN: 0 563 34408 3
Hardback ISBN: 0 563 34407 5

Printed in Great Britain by BPCC Paulton Books Limited

Typeset by TDR Photoset, Dartford, England
Origination by RCS Graphics Limited

Picture credits

cover (top right) Steve Pollock (bottom left) Tony Potter **p3** Steve Pollock **p10** Tony Potter **p12** Sally and Richard Greenhill **p13** Oxfam **p14** Rick Morris **p15** Sally and Richard Greenhill **p18** Trish Parker/Oxfam **p25** View As/NHPA **p34** John Wright **p35** (top,left) S. Krasemann/NHPA (top right) Steve Pollock **p38** Nigel Dennis/NHPA **p39** S. Robinson/NHPA **p45** Steve Pollock